TEACHING BEYOND THE CHALKBOARD

TEACHING BEYOND THE CHALKBOARD

A 21-Day Devotional for Teachers

IESHA SHAW
and
MARY SHAW

Limits of Liability and Disclaimer of Warranty

The author and publisher shall not be liable for your misuse of this material. This book is strictly for informational purposes. The purpose of this book is to educate and entertain. The author and publisher do not guarantee anyone following these techniques, suggestions, tips, ideas, or strategies will become successful. The author and publisher shall have neither liability nor responsibility to anyone with respect to any loss or damage caused, or alleged to be caused, directly or indirectly by the information contained in this book. Views expressed in this publication do not necessarily reflect the views of the publisher.

Printed in the United States of America
Keen Vision Publishing, LLC
www.publishwithKVP.com
ISBN: 978-1-955316-13-2

For teachers working hard every day to provide a great learning experience for their students. May God continue to give you strength as you cultivate the leaders of tomorrow.

CONTENTS

INTRODUCTION

As a young child, I experienced many challenges in school. Due to medical issues, I suffered from constant seizures. In the first grade, my parents and teachers decided that I needed to repeat the year so that I could retain more information and be better prepared for second grade. Unfortunately, being retained meant that I wouldn't get to move on with the classmates I'd known since pre-k. Adjusting to new classmates who weren't as understanding of my medical condition was very difficult.

As I got older, my health condition persisted. Throughout elementary school, I encountered many different types of teachers. Some were very understanding and helped me to succeed. Others were sometimes rude and didn't want to deal with the challenges my medical condition presented. In fifth grade, things started to take a turn for the worse. In addition to medical issues, teenage hormones, and other circumstances, I begin to battle with depression. Throughout fifth and sixth grade, I simply went to school because I had to. I had no desire to be in school.

My experience with school remained pretty consistent throughout 7th and 12th grade. I encountered supportive teachers who were very patient with me. However, I also had a few teachers who lacked the patience to help me learn, made it clear that they only taught for the paycheck, and lacked control over their classroom. When I had teachers like this, it made my learning experience even more dreadful. Overall, I was happy when I graduated and exited the world of school.

After graduating high school, I knew I wanted to do something to positively impact the lives of children. So I began pursuing a degree in early childhood education. I also began working with younger children. My experience as a student taught me some very valuable things about education. My heart and my passion are to impact young children's lives and help them love education.

I wrote this book as a source of inspiration and encouragement for those responsible for shaping the lives of children every day. Being a teacher is not always an easy task. Children are different, and they all have individual needs. However, a teacher is only one person, and sometimes it can be hard to meet the needs of every child in the classroom. A teacher's salary isn't enough for everything a teacher endures daily. For this reason, one who chooses the profession of teaching must have pure love and genuine passion for the work that is required. Even though teaching children is difficult, it is rewarding. If done correctly, teaching can have a lasting positive impact on children's lives.

Personally, I can vividly remember every teacher who

lovingly helped me succeed in the classroom. They taught me things that go beyond textbooks. Their influence in my life made me a better person. I am forever grateful for them. The purpose of this book is to remind teachers of their role in every student's life. It goes far beyond the chalkboard. After reading this devotional, I pray that teachers will be encouraged and inspired to make a positive impact in their students' lives beyond instruction and academics.

Day One

BEGIN WITH LOVE

"For God so loved the world, that he gave his only Son, that whoever believes in him should not perish but have eternal life."

John 3:16

Teachers have a big responsibility. The truth is, you can earn every degree available, but it still won't prepare you for the job of being a teacher. Students need more than reading, writing, and arithmetic. Though instruction is very important, a lot more goes into a child's education experience. Teachers must always be willing to encourage students when they don't feel confident. Teachers have to understand a child's personality and how it impacts their ability to learn. Teachers must know how to push children in a supportive and patient way. It is impossible to do any of this without love.

God is love, and as His children, we must give love as well. John 3:16 shows us that God's love for us is so powerful that He gave His only Son so that we will have eternal life. This scripture reminds us that love is all about our willingness to sacrifice.

As teachers, in order to make a positive impact in your students' lives, you must love them. Love your students enough to sacrifice your frustration so that they can learn. Love your students enough to sacrifice your way of doing things if it will help them learn better. Love your students enough to sacrifice time to hear their concerns or simply be a shoulder they can cry on.

Just as adults go through difficult things, children experience challenges as well. Sometimes, all they need is the love and support of their teacher to encourage them to keep going. As you prepare to teach, ask yourself, "What will my love for my students push me to do today?"

A TEACHER'S PRAYER

God,

Please help me to love my students like you do. Give me the strength to make a positive impact on their lives. Help me to be there for them and support them as they learn and grow. Amen.

JOURNALING

Use the lines to journal how you will use today's devotional inspiration to teach beyond the chalkboard.

Day Two

BE LED BY GOD

"All your children shall be taught by the Lord, and great shall be the peace of your children."

Isaiah 54:13

As children of God, we learn from Him. God teaches us through the experiences that we have every day. Our challenges teach us to trust God more. Blessings teach us how to be good stewards. Growth teaches us how to become more like Christ.

Even though we all may experience the same challenges, blessings, and growth, the way God teaches us in our situations may be different. Why? Because God knows that each of His children is different. We all require something different to learn from Him. God doesn't force us all to learn the same way. Instead, He gives us lessons based on our personalities, character, and what we need in order to learn.

In the same way, as teachers, we must be intentional about understanding what our students need in order to learn and grow. I know you may be wondering, "How do I teach every student differently? There are 20 of them and only 1 of me!" I definitely understand, and it can be overwhelming at times. However, this is when you must lean in and trust God to show you the best way to meet the needs of every student in your class.

Meeting the individual needs of students can be overwhelming. This is why you must always start your day with God. Even though prayer isn't allowed in school, you can pray in your car or silently at your desk. Ask God to give you the strength to be what your students need. Listen for God to give you wisdom when you are working with your students. Be patient with your students and with yourself. You don't have to be perfect in order to be a good teacher. You only have to be willing to trust God to guide you through making a positive impact in the lives of your students.

A TEACHER'S PRAYER

God,

I want to be led by you when dealing with my students. Give me the wisdom I need to teach them and meet their needs. Help me to be patient with every student, teacher, and parent I come in contact with. Amen.

JOURNALING

Use the lines to journal how you will use today's devotional inspiration to teach beyond the chalkboard.

Day Three

TEACHERS CARE

"By this all people will know that you are my disciples, if you have love for one another."

John 13:35

No matter their age, teaching children should start with a foundation of love, care, and support. The process of building a caring foundation with students should not be overlooked. On the first day of school, many teachers start with the classroom rules, letting students know what is expected of them and maybe a few conversations about what students did over the summer. How different do you think classrooms would be if teachers started the school year building a foundation of love, care, and support with their students?

Many students have difficult home life challenges. They may be raised in a home with single parents, many siblings, or low socioeconomic statuses. Even children who are raised in healthy home environments have challenges. This is why it is important for teachers to build good relationships with their students.

When you think about it, students spend more time in school than anywhere else, which means that the teacher spends a lot of time with students. Students need to know that their teachers care about them beyond their schoolwork. Students need teachers that also care about their physical, emotional, and mental wellbeing. It is easier for students to grow cognitively when they feel safe and supported.

There are many ways you can help your students feel safe in the classroom. Watch them closely as they play and interact with each other to ensure no one is being bullied or teased. When students have concerns, listen to them instead of brushing them off. If students get in trouble, be kind as you redirect them. Never speak harshly to your students or call them out of their names. If a student seems to be having a difficult time learning, don't make them feel bad. Instead, find a way to get them the support they need. When students seem distracted or worried, find a way to talk with them and find out what is going on with them. These are just a few suggestions to create a healthy environment in your classroom.

As teachers, we don't care just because we want to be good teachers. The Bible tells us that the love and care we show others is how people will recognize us as disciples of God. It's not about your degrees, how high your students' test scores are, or even how many teaching awards you gain. As a believer of God, you should strive to show your students how much you care and allow the light of Christ to shine through you.

A TEACHER'S PRAYER

God,

I want to show my students that I care about them. Help me to create a learning environment that allows Your light and love to shine through me. Amen.

JOURNALING

Use the lines on the next page to journal how you will use today's devotional inspiration to teach beyond the chalkboard.

Day Four

TEACHERS SUPPORT TEACHERS

"For if they fall, one will lift up his fellow. But woe to him who is alone when he falls and has not another to lift him up!"

Ecclesiastes 4:10

Donnie McClurkin's song, "We Fall Down," is one of my favorite songs. It is such a universal song that anyone can listen to and be encouraged by. The truth of the matter is, we all fall or fail sometimes. The beautiful thing is that God doesn't desire us to stay down. He is more than willing to help us get back up again.

One of God's favorite ways to help us get back up again is through other people. We were placed on this earth to build relationships with each other, not to do life alone. Our scripture today reminds us of the importance of working together and supporting others. Being a teacher is tough work, and no teacher should try to do it alone. Today, ask yourself, "How is my relationship with other teachers?" Every teacher, no matter where or how they teach, should have a community of teachers for support. No one understands the role of a teacher like other teachers. Challenge yourself to build relationships with other educators. Needing the help or assistance of other teachers doesn't make you a bad teacher. It makes you a smarter and stronger resource for your students.

When you need ideas to assist a child experiencing difficulty, another teacher can provide you with fresh ideas and things you may not have tried. When you need new ideas or activities for your class, another teacher may be able to share things they have done with their class. It is very helpful to have the support and assistance of other teachers. Don't forget to return the favor and support others when they are in need as well.

Teachers should never tear each other down, gossip about each other, or be unkind. Being a teacher is hard enough.

We shouldn't make the job harder by being harsh to each other. Allowing your students to see you working with other teachers sets a good example for them. They will learn how important it is to work with others and mimic your behavior in the classroom with other students.

A TEACHER'S PRAYER

God,
Thank you for putting people in my life to help me be a better teacher. Remind me to ask for help when I need it. Give me the strength to support other teachers when they are in need.

JOURNALING

Use the lines to journal how you will use today's devotional inspiration to teach beyond the chalkboard.

Day Five

TRAIN THEM UP

"Train up a child in the way he should go; even when he is old he will not depart from it."

Proverbs 22:6

A large problem with the world we live in today is how children were raised and are being raised. Many of the adults who run the world today weren't raised in a way that is pleasing to God. This is why there are so many adults who are unkind, rude and make bad decisions. Though we can't go back and change the past, we can do better in the future.

Children aren't able to raise themselves. Adults often get frustrated or overwhelmed with children when they do not behave nicely. However, this is typical for children because they are still learning and developing. This is why everyone must be intentional about raising and steering children in the correct path.

Many teachers complain about student's behavior and say that it is the parent's responsibility to raise them. While this is true, this should not keep teachers from setting standards and expectations for students in the classroom. Some children aren't taught how to respect others and obey instructions. This does not mean that you, as a teacher, have to allow poor behavior in your classroom. Redirect students who are misbehaving. Teach them the correct way to treat others and how to respect adults.

You may not have control over what students do at home, but you can control what you allow to happen in your classroom. Be loving and kind to students, and teach them how they should behave. For some students, your classroom may be the only place where they learn how to treat others.

Instead of being frustrated with the student or even the parents, pray for them and ask God to show you how to deal with these types of students. Pray that God will allow the training your students receive in your classroom to become a part of their lives.

A TEACHER'S PRAYER

God,

Please help me to deal with the different issues my students may have. Guide me as I train them in the way they should go. Give me patience, wisdom and strength to discipline them with love.

JOURNALING

Use the lines to journal how you will use today's devotional inspiration to teach beyond the chalkboard.

Day Six

CHRIST IS YOUR STRENGTH

"I can do all things through Christ who strengthens me."

Philippians 4:13

This scripture is one of my favorites because it is very encouraging! Today, allow this scripture to encourage you to get through your day as a teacher. Sometimes, the work of a teacher can be stressful. There are many days when a teacher has to be the parent, nurse, referee, janitor, and chef in the classroom … in addition to being the teacher. When it feels like you can't go any further and you want to throw in the towel, take a deep breath and remember that you can do all things through Christ!

God is pleased with the work that teachers do. He is proud of you for choosing such a selfless job. You could be anywhere in the world, doing whatever you desire to do, but you decided to train up the next generation of leaders. Know that God can and will be your strength. When your classroom feels like it is all over the place, take a moment to pray and ask God to help you through the day.

In addition to teachers needing encouragement, sometimes students need encouragement too. Remember, they are little humans, and though their problems may seem small to you, their issues are BIG to them. So when you see students who are overwhelmed or sad, spend some time encouraging them as well.

Some teachers say nasty things to students in the heat of the moment. What teachers must realize is that students will remember those words forever. So, instead of pointing out how "bad" a student may be, try encouraging them the same way you would want to be encouraged if you were having a rough day.

With a bit of encouragement, we can make the world a better place. As a teacher, allow the Word of God to encourage you so that you can encourage the students God has trusted you to teach.

A TEACHER'S PRAYER

God,

I need your strength to teach. You know everything that I deal with everyday. Encourage my heart so that I can encourage students. Amen.

JOURNALING

Use the lines to journal how you will use today's devotional inspiration to teach beyond the chalkboard.

Day Seven

STAY POSITIVE

"Finally, brothers, whatever is true, whatever is honorable, whatever is just, whatever is pure, whatever is lovely, whatever is commendable, if there is any excellence, if there is anything worthy of praise, think about these things."

Philippians 4:8

From my experience working with children, I've learned that you must remain positive in order to make a positive impact in their lives. This requires you to be honest, pure, loving, and have a great rapport with your students, parents, and other teachers. Our scripture focus for today reminds us to keep our minds on things that are true, honest, fair, pure, lovely, and good.

Teachers often get so frustrated with their tasks that they become very negative about their job, students, parents, and even other teachers. We must remember that we will have whatever we think about or say. If you wake up every morning expecting a rough day at work, you will have a rough day. If you speak negative things about your students, they will continue to act negatively. Our world is shaped by our thoughts, actions, and words. This is why Paul reminds us in Philippians 4:8 to think about the positive things. Making this adjustment will shift your entire day in the classroom.

Students love to work with teachers who are kind and positive. These teachers are more successful with working with students than teachers who are mean, rude, and negative. When a student knows that you are positive and joyful about teaching, they will open up to you, do what you ask them to do with a smile, and work very hard.

Parents also enjoy working with kind teachers. Some parents can be difficult to work with. However, as a teacher, you must remain positive. Your positivity has the power to change the heart and mindset of difficult parents.

Finally, teachers are always excited to support other teachers who are positive. No one wants to work with someone who is always negative or speaking down about things. So be sure that you don't vent to your co-teachers. Try to focus on the positive and always look for the good in things.

Being a teacher comes with its trials and tribulations. Every day isn't always sunny. However, even on the rough days, try to find something positive about the day. It will drastically improve your reputation with students, parents, and other teachers. With a good reputation, a teacher can make a good impact on the lives of students.

A TEACHER'S PRAYER

God,

Staying positive can be hard. When things are going crazy in my life and in my classroom, remind me to think about the positive things. Give me the ability to see the sunshine, even on rainy days. Amen.

JOURNALING

Use the lines to journal how you will use today's devotional inspiration to teach beyond the chalkboard.

Day Eight

CHILDREN ARE GIFTS

"Children are a gift from the Lord; they are a reward from him."

Psalm 127:3

How do you view your students? Do you see them as a job that needs to be done so that you can get paid? Do you see them as a grade or a test score? Do you see them according to their good or bad behavior? This scripture makes it very clear how God sees children, and ultimately, how we should see every student that walks into our classrooms. They are a gift and a reward from the Lord.

Every student in your classroom was placed there on purpose by God. God placed those students in your path because He trusts you to develop them for their future. It is very difficult to positively impact children's lives if you don't see them the way God sees them. Many teachers miss the opportunity to make a good deposit in their students' lives because they don't see their students correctly.

Don't get me wrong. I know that some days, children can be a handful. Sometimes they are loud, rude, disobedient, and even unkind. However, this does not change the fact that they are a gift from God. As a teacher, you must be intentional not to view children based on how they act at the moment. If you make this mistake, you will label a child. When children are given labels, it makes it very hard for them to become something different. As a teacher, you should always be optimistic that every child can learn and grow. Honestly, if you don't believe this, you've chosen the wrong job, and you will do more harm than good in the lives of your students.

Many children suffer from low self-esteem. They see themselves according to the shoes their parents can afford, how popular they are with other students, who sits with them at lunch, and even who plays with them during recess. As a teacher, you have the opportunity to help children increase their self-esteem. However, it is hard to do this if you don't see students as gifts from God.

Think about this. What do you do when you receive a gift or a reward from someone? Most of the time, you take good care of it. You are grateful for it. You try your best to steward it well. Think of your students the same way. God has given you the gift of teaching, and He has blessed you with amazing students to teach. When days are rough, and it seems like all of your students had too much candy, take a deep breath and remind yourself that they are a gift from God. Changing your view of your students will help you care for them properly. When you allow yourself to be grateful for the opportunity to teach them, you will teach with passion and excitement. As you view your students as gifts from God, you will steward them well and give your all to ensure they are successful.

Finally, parents can always tell how a teacher feels about their student. If a parent feels that you have a positive view of their student, they will trust your wisdom, insight, and instruction. Trust is a major component in the parent/teacher relationship. When parents and teachers have a good relationship, students do even better in class.

A TEACHER'S PRAYER

God,

Today, help me remember that children are a gift from You. Show me how to make them feel special, important, loved, cared for, and heard. Amen.

JOURNALING

Use the lines to journal how you will use today's devotional inspiration to teach beyond the chalkboard.

Day Nine

LET THEM SEE CHRIST IN YOU

"But Jesus said, "Let the little children come to me and do not hinder them, for to such belongs the kingdom of heaven."

Matthew 19:14

As believers, we know how important it is to raise our children to believe in Jesus Christ. In most public schools, teachers are not able to teach children about God or share Christ with them. This does not mean that you still cannot exhibit Christ to your students. So, how can teachers show Christ to students in schools where religion is not allowed? You let your actions do the talking!

There are students who live in rough neighborhoods or places where people do not operate in a Christian manner. In your classroom, they should have the opportunity to see something different from the community they live in.

Show children the love of Christ by teaching them in a way that is pleasing to Him. Before you say something to a student, ask yourself how God feels about what you are going to say. Furthermore, ask yourself how your words may impact the student. If your words do not uplift and redirect the student to success, you probably shouldn't say it.

Very often, Christians work hard to show the love of Christ in church, but that is not the only place where we should be Christ-like. God wants us to let our light shine in every place in the world, even in places where talking about God is not allowed. That is how the testimony of God's love is spread throughout the earth. We must be willing to be a representation of Christ no matter where we are.

As a teacher, every time you choose to treat your students with love and respect, you allow your light to shine. When you pray for your students before you get to school, you let your light shine. When you use kind and positive words, you allow your students to see Christ. Don't allow a negative attitude, bad words, or impatience to make you dim your light. The best way to show your students Christ is to operate as a believer should in every circumstance.

Finally, pray for your students. In many schools, teachers can talk about religion with students or pray with students if they request it or bring it up. Find out your school's rules about religion. Pray that God will use you to be a light in the lives of your students and their parents. Ask God to send people into their lives to teach them about the love of Christ. Whatever you do, don't hinder students from seeing Christ through you every day. Their interaction with you can be the very thing that leads them to a relationship with Jesus Christ. Every day, remind yourself that you are the light and salt of the world. You have a responsibility to allow the light of Christ to shine everywhere you go, especially in your classroom.

A TEACHER'S PRAYER

God,
Use me as a light in the lives of my students and their parents. Stir up a desire in them to learn more about you. Remind me daily that you have called me to be the salt and the light in the world. Show me how to shine your light for all to see You. Amen.

JOURNALING

Use the lines on the next page to journal how you will use today's devotional inspiration to teach beyond the chalkboard.

Day Ten

YOUR WORK IS NOT IN VAIN

"Therefore, my beloved brothers, be steadfast, immovable, always abounding in the work of the Lord, knowing that in the Lord your labor is not in vain."

1 Corinthians 15:58

Today, I want to encourage you to be unmovable in the work God has anointed you to do in the lives of children. Being a teacher can be challenging, but being a good teacher is hard work! Sometimes, it can feel like the work you are doing isn't making a difference. It feels like you teach, love, and care, but the students still aren't getting it. When you start to feel discouraged, it's natural to consider throwing in the towel or giving up. There may even be days when you don't feel like being encouraging; you just want the children to act right, pass the test, or be kind to each other.

Be encouraged, teacher! Know that the work you are doing is not in vain. You may not see the proof just yet, but know that it is on the way. One thing you probably didn't know was that teachers are also gardeners. Every time you teach, you are planting a seed in your student's minds. Each time you stay after school to tutor a struggling student, you are planting seeds. Whenever you choose to listen to a student's problems or issues, you are planting a seed. Right when you least expect it, those seeds will sprout up and grow!

The challenging thing about being a teacher is understanding that every child's growth process is different. Some students grow rapidly, while others take a little longer to grow or understand. Be okay if you try your hardest but still don't see growth in your students during the school year. Trust and believe that everything you are planting in them will grow in due time.

As you continue to plant with love and care, remember that you are working unto the Lord. Even if you don't see a reward in test scores or students' behavior, God will reward you for your hard work. Stand firm. Don't give up. Submit your work unto the Lord. Continue to pray for your students, parents, and yourself. Lean on God daily and depend on His strength. You got this!

A TEACHER'S PRAYER

God,
I believe that I am making a difference in the lives of my students. When the days are tough, remind me that I am working unto you and that my work is not in vain. Amen.

JOURNALING

Use the lines to journal how you will use today's devotional inspiration to teach beyond the chalkboard.

Day Eleven

SEE FOR YOURSELF

"Let no one deceive you with empty words, for because of these things the wrath of God comes upon the sons of disobedience."

Ephesians 5:6

Before the first day of school, many teachers sit down to discuss returning students. They share their previous experience with students with each other in hopes of starting the first day of school with no surprises. While it is great for teachers to help each other prepare for new students, be careful not to expect negative things from students just because of their previous experience with another teacher.

Today, take a look at every student in your classroom. Ask yourself if your perspective of them was based on something another teacher said or your true observation of them. Like adults, students also need the space to grow and change. How would you feel if people still expected the old you every time you tried to turn over a new leaf or change your life? You would probably be very frustrated or irritated. You may even feel like trying to start over is pointless. Don't allow your students to feel the same way. Discern the information other teachers share about students.

Many factors play into the experience a teacher has with a student. For instance, their teaching style, classroom management, and even personality can be factors in a teacher's relationship with students. Be careful not to allow one teacher's opinion of a student to become your truth. Instead, learn the student for yourself, and seek God for wisdom on dealing with that student.

Remember, children grow at their own unique pace. Be sure that your classroom is a place where students can grow, change, and succeed. Challenge yourself to expect positive changes in your students every day. If they have a bad day on Monday, allow them to start Tuesday with a fresh slate.

When you expect positive growth from your students, you will see positive growth. However, if you expect them to remain the same, they will remain the same.

A TEACHER'S PRAYER

God,

Teach me how to expect positive changes in my students. Erase any idea of them that I have because of someone else's experience with them. Amen.

JOURNALING

Use the lines to journal how you will use today's devotional inspiration to teach beyond the chalkboard.

Day Twelve

CORRECT WITH LOVE

"Whoever spares the rod hates his son, but he who loves him is diligent to discipline him."

Proverbs 13:24

When done correctly, discipline can show students how much you love and care for them. Believe it or not, students love structure. They like classrooms where there is a schedule, rules, and expectations. When classrooms are out of order, messy, and confusing, it is very difficult for students to learn and grow. In your classroom, be sure that there is order and that you teach your students discipline. Many schools do not allow teachers to discipline children physically. However, teachers must understand that physical punishment is not the only way or the best way to discipline students. When students do not obey the rules or instructions you have given, you must be sure to let the student know what they have done wrong. Many teachers are passive-aggressive and may ignore students when they do something incorrectly. Ignoring poor behavior is not a healthy way to discipline students, and it also does not allow them to learn from their mistakes.

When students do things that you disapprove of, take a moment to breathe and assess the situation. When we are disappointed with students, the first thing that comes to our minds is not the best thing to say. It is best to wait until you have calmed down before disciplining a student. Once you are cool, calm, and collected, let the student know what they have done wrong and explain the consequences of their actions. Allow their consequence to be something that allows them the opportunity to think about what they have done wrong and how they plan to correct their behavior the next time. Be sure to let them know you are not punishing them but allowing them to think about their actions.

As a teacher, you play a significant role in the training of your students. Don't ignore students when they do something wrong. There are times where a student's misbehavior can be a cry for help or attention. Address the students in a kind and loving way. Use every opportunity to discipline your students as a way to show how much you care about their future success.

A TEACHER'S PRAYER

God,
Children need discipline and direction in order to become what you desire them to be. Guide me in disciplining them with love. Help them to improve their behavior and treat others with respect. Amen.

JOURNALING

Use the lines to journal how you will use today's devotional inspiration to teach beyond the chalkboard.

Day Thirteen

PARENTS & TEACHERS UNITE

"Two are better than one, because they have a good reward for their toil."

Ecclesiastes 4:9

Welcome to Day Thirteen! I hope you have been enjoying this devotional so far. Today, I want to encourage you to build strong relationships with your students' parents. There is a lot of power in strong parent and teacher relationships. Training children is not a job for just one person. It takes the entire community to teach children the way that they should go. Teachers are a large part of that community, and it is very important that teachers begin to see themselves as a part of the child's community.

Sometimes, adults can be harder to work with than children! All teachers will say, "AMEN!" to that. However, teachers must always try their best to foster a healthy relationship with parents. No one knows children better than their parents/guardians. Building a good relationship with parents can help you understand the child better, learn what approaches work for them, see their personality traits, and comprehend the home environment students are raised in. Simply having a conversation with parents about their students can make a major difference in a student's classroom success.

When students know that their parents and teachers are working together to ensure their success, they feel loved, cared for, and supported. This will result in an improvement in their classroom behavior and academic performance.

Teachers, I know sometimes it feels like you have to push students alone, but you don't. Find a few ways to include parents in your students' learning experiences. Yes, some parents work a lot and may not have time to attend a lot of parent/teacher conferences, but find a way to work with them. As you foster relationships with parents, you may even find a few parents who wouldn't mind helping with things in the classroom, donating class supplies, or providing cool activities for your class. There are so many great opportunities in parent/teacher relationships.

A TEACHER'S PRAYER

God,
Please help me to love my students like you do. Give me the strength to make a positive impact on their lives. Help me to be there for them and support them as they learn and grow. Amen.

JOURNALING

Use the lines to journal how you will use today's devotional inspiration to teach beyond the chalkboard.

Day Fourteen

TAKE CARE OF YOURSELF

"For no one ever hated his own flesh, but nourishes and cherishes it, just as Christ does the church."

Ephesians 5:29

When was the last time you did something you enjoy, like going to see a movie, having dinner with friends, or getting a massage? As a teacher, you experience a lot of stress. You care for students, communicate with parents, prepare lessons, and work extremely hard to ensure your students' success. This can be very tiring. In order to do your job with love and care, you must take care of yourself.

Many teachers around the world teach even when they don't feel good, are tired, or feel overwhelmed. This usually leads to a classroom that is tense and not filled with love or excitement about learning. Today, I want to encourage you to take care of yourself. You can only be a great teacher to your students if you are good to yourself. Instead of grading papers or doing lesson plans every weekend, schedule time to do something relaxing and healthy. You deserve to be well, and teaching does not have to be a daunting task. When you aren't feeling well, utilize your sick days, stay home, and take care of yourself. There is no point in attempting to teach students when you are sick.

Also, find a way to take small breaks throughout your day, even if you take five minutes just to look out of the window and breathe. Doing small things like this will ensure that you don't get too frustrated as you are teaching the future leaders of tomorrow.

I know that you have many things to do. However, you won't do those things well if you don't take care of yourself. You may be afraid of your students getting behind on learning if you have to request a sub for a day or two, but don't allow that fear to keep you from taking care of yourself. Remember that God has your back, and He is helping you on your quest to make a positive impact in the lives of your students. Trust that while you are resting or taking care of yourself at home, God is taking care of your students at school.

When teachers are healthy, well-rested, and stress-free, they can do amazing things for their students. Remember, you deserve to rest and take care of yourself. Self-care isn't selfish. It ensures that you are able to continue doing what you do for others!

A TEACHER'S PRAYER

God,

I desire to be my best so that I can help my students be their best. Remind me to take care of myself. Show me how to manage my time so that I can care for myself and stay healthy and strong. Amen.

JOURNALING

Use the lines to journal how you will use today's devotional inspiration to teach beyond the chalkboard.

Day Fifteen

START THE DAY RIGHT

"O Lord, in the morning you hear my voice; in the morning I prepare a sacrifice for you and watch."

Psalm 5:3

What do you do to prepare for the day? Do you jump out of bed, get dressed, check your emails, and run out of the door? Many people start their day this way. As a result, they often feel overwhelmed and tired as the day progresses. How we start our day plays a big part in how successful our day will be. As teachers, our work begins the minute we get out of the car and walk into the school. In order to be prepared, we must have a positive, healthy, and inspiring morning routine. Here are a few things every teacher should include in their morning routine:

PRAYER, MEDITATION, OR DEVOTION

Starting your day with quiet time is a great way to focus and prepare your mind. You can pray, listen to worship music, read the Bible, or even listen to an inspiring message from your favorite speaker. Doing this will give you the encouragement you need to make it through the day. As the day progresses, you may encounter challenges with students, parents, or other teachers. When difficulty arises, you can remember your time in prayer, a scripture you read, or something encouraging you heard in a song or a message.

NOURISHMENT

Breakfast is the most important meal of the day. Even when we sleep, our bodies burn energy. When you wake up, it is very important to fuel your body with healthy food. Eating a healthy breakfast will allow you to be alert and ready for the day. Most people who don't eat breakfast feel sluggish or tired before lunchtime. Challenge yourself to wake up early enough to eat a nutritious meal before you head into the classroom. Your students will be full of energy! Eating a healthy breakfast will ensure that you are able to keep up with them!

SELF-CARE

You deserve to take care of yourself every day. Don't just wait for the weekend to care for yourself. Be sure to groom yourself and put on fresh clothes before you run out of the door for work. When you look good, you feel good, and when you feel good, you are able to do good work! Taking care of yourself in the morning is vital to a successful day with your students.

BREATHE!

Sometimes, teachers have so much to do that they forget to take deep breaths. Take a deep breath before you dive into teaching your students, grading papers, meetings, and other educator tasks. Breathing recenters you and helps you relax. If you are on edge and stressed, your students will be able to tell, and you won't be as patient or kind with them. However, when a teacher is relaxed, it sets a calm tone for the entire class.

If you don't have a healthy morning routine, challenge yourself to begin one today! Remember, how you start your day determines the success of your day.

A TEACHER'S PRAYER

God,

Show me how to start my day correctly. Throughout the day, remind me to breathe and talk with you. I believe that with your help, I can start and finish each day strong. Amen.

JOURNALING

Use the lines to journal how you will use today's devotional inspiration to teach beyond the chalkboard.

Day Sixteen

DON'T WORRY

"Do not be anxious about anything, but in everything by prayer and supplication with thanksgiving let your requests be made known to God. And the peace of God, which surpasses all understanding, will guard your hearts and your minds in Christ Jesus."

Philippians 4:6-7

Teachers all across the world battle with anxiety and stress. No one understands the pressure teachers are under quite like other teachers. To people who don't teach, it may appear that the job of a teacher is easy. However, those who are determined to make a positive impact in the lives of their students know that teaching can be a challenging task. In addition to all the requirements of the school or the organization, teachers have to ensure that children are safe, cared for, heard, and given the best opportunity to succeed. No matter how hard we try, it can feel like nothing we do is working some days. This can lead to anxiety and worry.

Our scripture focus for today reminds us not to be anxious about anything. Of course, this is easier said than done. When students are staring you in the face, piles of papers need to be graded, and your email is filled with information from parents and administration, it's easy to stress and become overwhelmed. However, God tells us what to do when anxiety presents itself. Philippians 4:6-7 tells us that this is the perfect time to pray.

Anxiety and worry melt away when we pray to God because we are reminded that God has our back. Instead of trying to do everything in our own strength, we should stop, pray, and ask God for what we need. Prayer also gives us the opportunity to remember that God is bigger than any storm we may face. When we pray, we give our burdens and problems over to God. He is more than able to carry us through any challenges.

My favorite part about this scripture is that God promises to grant us peace. This means that even though our problems may not be solved yet, we will have peace as God works everything out on our behalf.

A TEACHER'S PRAYER

God,

When I am tempted to worry, remind me to pray. I submit my requests to you this morning. I believe you will allow your peace to fill my heart and my classroom. Amen.

JOURNALING

Use the lines to journal how you will use today's devotional inspiration to teach beyond the chalkboard.

Day Seventeen

WATCH YOUR MOUTH

"Death and life are in the power of the tongue: and they that love it shall eat the fruit thereof."

Proverbs 18:21

When I was in grade school, I often heard teachers say unkind things to students. I've heard teachers tell students that they would never be anything. I've even heard teachers tell students that they would be just like their parents or siblings who were not successful in life. Even though students would respond as if they did not care what the teacher said, the truth of the matter is, they did care. Words like that hurt and remain in the minds and memories of students for the rest of their lives.

In addition to saying mean things to students, I also recall teachers walking into the classroom with a negative attitude, saying things like, "I know you all are going to act up today, but if you do, you will be going straight to the principal's office. I am not going to put up with any foolishness for today." Sure enough, students would misbehave, the classroom would be loud, and no one would learn anything.

As teachers, we must always remember the power in the words we speak. We can use our words to push our students to success, or we can use our words to push them into failure. Our words can shift the classroom into a healthy and fun learning environment, or our words can make school a place that children hate.

Today, I want to challenge you to speak words of positivity to your students. Be mindful of the things that you allow to come out of your mouth when you are upset, frustrated, or overwhelmed. Students act according to what we expect. If we say negative things about them, they will continue to act that way and even get worse. Speaking down to children does not push them to be successful. It does the complete opposite. Starting your day with negative words does not ensure that students will not misbehave. Instead, it shapes the tone of the class for the day.

As a believer, you have a responsibility to speak the things that are not as though they are. You must allow your words to be filled with faith, hope, and optimism. When you speak as a believer in your classroom, it will change everything.

So what are you waiting for? Today, use your words to push your students towards their bright future. When they are older, they will remember the words you spoke over them. Make sure that those words are positive and encouraging.

A TEACHER'S PRAYER

God,
Help me to encourage and uplift my students every day. Guide me to use kind words when I talk to them. Amen.

JOURNALING

Use the lines to journal how you will use today's devotional inspiration to teach beyond the chalkboard.

____

____

____

____

____

____

Day Eighteen

DO YOUR BEST

"Whatever you do, work heartily, as for the Lord and not for men, knowing that from the Lord you will receive the inheritance as your reward. You are serving the Lord Christ."

Colossians 3:23-24

One thing that made me dislike school was teachers who obviously did not enjoy teaching. In high school, I had several teachers who did not teach us anything. Instead, they gave us textbooks and made us write all day. The class wasn't engaging, we didn't have fun projects or assignments to do, and we didn't talk about the information that we wrote. This allowed students to have the opportunity to talk, misbehave, and even tease other children. When students aren't engaged, they will become bored and disinterested in class. When students are bored, they will do things to create excitement.

As teachers, we have control over our classroom and our students' learning experiences. Even though we will have days where everyone is exhausted and may not feel like doing too much, this should not be an everyday habit. When you agreed to be a teacher, you didn't just agree to give students a bunch of information. You signed up to create a learning environment that helps students love education and improve themselves.

Today, take some time and think about the learning experience you are providing your students. Are you doing just enough to get by? Do you only focus on making sure students are able to pass tests? If so, think about how you can make learning fun for each student. One way to do this is to think about your students' interests. What do they like to do? What gets them excited? Find ways to implement these fun activities in the learning process.

When students are engaged in their learning, they will want to learn more. Instead of hating school, they will be excited about coming to school each day. Many teachers think that it is the student's fault if they don't like to learn.

This is not true. Many students don't like to learn because of the experiences that they have had with teachers and school. You can make a difference in your students' lives by ensuring that your classroom is a fun and safe environment for learning.

Teaching requires a lot of hard work, but remember to do everything unto God. Know that God will see the work you put in with your students and reward you for it! How do you think God feels about the work you do to help your students succeed? Are there things that you can do today to improve your students' learning experience?

A TEACHER'S PRAYER

God,

Help me to provide my students with a great learning experience. Give me fresh and fun ideas to help them learn. Grant me the strength to be creative and intentional. Amen.

JOURNALING

Use the lines to journal how you will use today's devotional inspiration to teach beyond the chalkboard.

Day Nineteen

HAVE FAITH

"Now faith is confidence in what we hope for and assurance about what we do not see."

Hebrews 11:1

Whether we know it or not, we use faith every day in small ways. For example, when we sit in a chair, we have faith that the chair will hold us. When we turn the faucet on, we have faith that water will begin to flow. When we walk into buildings, we have faith that the building will not collapse. When we drive, we have faith that the roads and bridges we cross will be able to hold our cars. Even though it seems small, we are exercising faith any time we expect things that we use every day to work correctly.

For teachers, faith is very important. Faith is the fuel we need to do anything well. Faith is what gives us the ability to believe that things will improve, even when we don't see evidence of it. Students come from all walks of life. They have different needs, challenges, and experiences. Sometimes, students struggle with their behavior and their academics. As teachers, our job is not to accept that students will always struggle in these areas. Instead, we should have faith that they will improve and get better.

As you get ready to teach students today, think about your faith in your students' success. Many teachers teach but do not believe in their students. Students can always tell if a teacher believes in them. How? Well, I'm glad you asked. Teachers who believe in their students talk, teach, and care for students differently from teachers who don't believe in their students. A teacher who has faith in their students' success will be kind, patient, understanding, and will work hard to help students succeed. A teacher who does not have faith in their students' ability to succeed won't put much effort into helping students succeed. Your faith level is the driving force behind your attitude when you teach and deal with students.

Pay close attention to your attitude towards your students today. If you have not been kind or very helpful to your students, you may need to address your faith in them. I know you may be wondering, "How can I have faith in my students when they are not improving?" Remember the definition of faith that we are given in our scripture for today. Faith is confidence in what we hope for. Do you hope that your student will succeed? Every good teacher should. Put your faith in God to help your students improve. Don't lean on your own understanding. Instead, seek God's wisdom and instruction.

When you have faith in your students, you will be able to honestly tell them that you believe in them. Having teachers believe in them increases students' confidence. Many students struggle with learning because they don't have confidence in themselves. Your faith in them can be the game-changer in their success.

Think about when you were a child. How did you feel when you knew someone believed in you? It probably made you want to work harder and give your best. So be sure to give the gift of hope to your students as well.

A TEACHER'S PRAYER

God,

Without faith, it is impossible to make a positive impact in the lives of my students. Give me the faith to push and inspire them to achieve great things! Amen.

JOURNALING

Use the lines to journal how you will use today's devotional inspiration to teach beyond the chalkboard.

Day Twenty

BE A SAFE PLACE

"Above all, keep loving one another earnestly, since love covers a multitude of sins. Show hospitality to one another without grumbling. As each has received a gift, use it to serve one another, as good stewards of God's varied grace."

1 Peter 4:8-10

Research shows us that many children battle things in silence. They never feel comfortable enough to share how they may be struggling. Even though they are young, children go through many things that teachers don't know about. They may be dealing with issues at home like domestic abuse, maltreatment, homelessness, poverty, or even molestation. They may be experiencing bullying, low self-confidence, difficulty making friends, or fear of failure at school. A lot of times, when children are battling issues, they don't know how to put their problems in words, or they may be afraid of getting in trouble for sharing what they are going through. For this reason, teachers must always make an effort to build a positive relationship with students and create a safe place for students to share how they feel.

Many adults make the mistake of making children feel like their feelings and emotions are not valid. They say things like, "Children should be seen, not heard." When children try to voice their opinion, they are ignored or told to be quiet. Ignoring children is not healthy because it tells the child that they do not have a voice. Silencing children can lead to children harming themselves or others because they are looking for attention or don't value their lives.

When I work with children, I try my best to get to know them beyond schoolwork. I play with them and do my best to make them feel comfortable with me. Small actions like this allow students to know that you are a safe place and that they can trust you to listen to them.

Think back to when you were a child. Were there moments when you wished you had someone to talk to? You may not be able to go back and change your childhood, but you can be to children what you wish someone was to you.

Today, challenge yourself to see your students beyond their test scores. How are they feeling? How do they respond to other children? Do they look well-kept? Do they appear to be sick or hurting? If you notice anything with your students, don't be afraid to ask them how they are doing or refer them to the school nurse. Your attentiveness to your students' wellbeing can be the very thing that saves their lives.

Every child you encounter is trying to find their place in the big world. They are still learning and growing. They need your assistance to adjust to the changes in the world around them.

A TEACHER'S PRAYER

God,

When I am busy with teacher tasks and duties, remind me to check on the students You have blessed me to teach. Grant me the strength to handle anything I may learn about my students. Amen.

JOURNALING

Use the lines to journal how you will use today's devotional inspiration to teach beyond the chalkboard.

Day Twenty - One

TEACHERS MAKE THE WORLD GO AROUND!

I believe that teachers have the most important jobs in the world. When you think about it, no one can ever become anything without teachers! How would we have doctors if there was no one to teach them? How would we have presidents and governors if no one taught them about law and policy? Every profession and career you can think of requires a teacher. So no matter what you get paid or your job's benefits, know that your role is important.

Every day, you get to play a role in the lives of the world's next great leaders. Sitting in your classroom can be the next great president, CEO, lawyer, doctor, nurse, cashier, fireman, or police officer. As a teacher, you have the opportunity to shape their minds and nurture their growth. Teaching is such a special responsibility, and only special people can do it.

Today, teacher, I want to remind you just how special you are. Everyone is not graced to do what you do every day. You could have been anything in the world, but you chose to be a teacher. Thank you so much for choosing to make a difference in the lives of children. Despite what your journey has been like, take some time today to appreciate the hard work you have done. Teaching is not easy, and we won't always get it right. As our students learn and grow, we are learning and growing. With effort, prayer, and hard work, we will improve every day.

Take the pressure off of yourself to be perfect. You will make mistakes as a teacher, and that is okay. After you have rough days, get up, dust yourself off, pray and try again. Whatever you do, do not give up.

This generation needs you more than ever! You have the power and the authority to turn your students' lives around for the better. With the help of God, you will make a positive impact in the lives of every child you encounter.

A TEACHER'S PRAYER

God,

Thank you for blessing me with the opportunity to be a teacher. As I continue to grow as a teacher, be with me. Remind me every day that what I am doing matters. Be my strength as I do what you have assigned me to do for your precious children. Amen.

JOURNALING

Use the lines to journal how you will use today's devotional inspiration to teach beyond the chalkboard.

STAY CONNECTED

Thank you for reading *Teaching Beyond the Chalkbooard*. Iesha would love to connect with you. Here are a few ways that you can connect with the author.

FACEBOOK Iesha Shaw
EMAIL shaw_iesha@yahoo.com

www.ingramcontent.com/pod-product-compliance
Lightning Source LLC
LaVergne TN
LVHW051812080426
835513LV00017B/1916